PRESSURE…

PAIN..

PROMISE.

A JOURNEY FROM DARKNESS TO DESTINY.

CARMALITA L. HAWKINS, J.D.

PRESSURE…

PAIN..

PROMISE.

A JOURNEY FROM DARKNESS TO DESTINY.

All Rights Reserved ©2016 by Kairos Consulting Group, LLC. Pressure…Pain..PROMISE. Is the exclusive property of Kairos Consulting Group, LLC. All rights reserved. No part of this book may be reproduced in any form or by electronic or mechanical means, including information storage and retrieval systems without the expressed permission in writing from the Publisher.

Published by:

Kairos Consulting Group, LLC

P.O. Box 14882

Tallahassee, FL. 32317

A JOURNEY FROM DARKNESS TO DESTINY

Cover & Book Design by:

Michael Cork of MaCork Solutions

www.Macorksolutions.com

Printed in the United States of America

ISBN 13: 978-1523215836

ISBN 10: 1523215836

PRESSURE...PAIN..PROMISE.

TABLE OF CONTENTS

Dedication..5

Introduction...7

Chapter 1 | PRESSURE...9

Chapter 2 | PRESSURE...20

Chapter 3 | PRESSURE...28

Chapter 4 | PAIN..38

Chapter 5 | PAIN..46

Chapter 6 | PAIN..61

Chapter 7 | PROMISE...72

Chapter 8 | PROMISE...78

Chapter 9 | PROMISE...85

Letter to the Adopted Children & Those in Foster Care......93

A JOURNEY FROM DARKNESS TO DESTINY

DEDICATION

This book is dedicated to my parents,

Lucille D. Hawkins & Cleveland Hawkins

who chose me at birth to love and raise as their own.

Although my Father passed away when I was eight years old,

I believe that he showed an abundance of love in the first eight years of my life, that many only dream of experiencing in a lifetime....

My mother, is my Angel on Earth

Because of her, I am here today.

The woman I am, the mother I will always strive to be

Is Because I grew up with a

Phenomenal Woman...

And She, is my Heart beat... Always.

To my children, **Cameron & Justice** who joined me on this journey. Their patience and strength through it all – loving me no less because of the Pressure, but in fact, loving me through my Pain and together, they kept me hopeful for a future Promise...They were my saving Grace...Many days I wanted to quit and end it all – but the thought of them, made me hold on and try again...and again...and again... And here we are.

I love you both beyond the moon.

PRESSURE...PAIN..PROMISE.

To my dearest sister and brother in Christ,

April Carter & **Christopher Parrish**

Who always encouraged me to write...

Who pushed me into my Purpose unapologetically and

kept me "on track" as much as they could!

I will always love you and thank God for this ordained and

Divine connection.

To my Mentor, **Mr. Wahid Shakur (Mr.Tycoon)** THANK YOU for reminding me daily who I was and who I was destined to be. You called me by my Future and not my Past, because of you, I kept my eyes on who I would one day become – even on the days

I couldn't "see it".

you always believed...For that, I am blessed to call you friend.

To my Spiritual Father, **Pastor Joseph Davis, Jr.**, THANK YOU for the series,

"Go Get Your Life" (2015)

Your on-time message catapulted me into my Gifts from God that were dormant for so very long... THANK YOU & **Pastor Robbin Davis**, for your constant prayer and guidance over my life and for believing in me. Even when I did not believe I was "good enough" or even "worthy", you chose me still to serve...which caused me to heal...and finally, tell my story.

To you both, I am eternally grateful.

INTRODUCTION

It didn't seem fair.

What was wrong with her?

Her big brown eyes full of innocence...

All fingers and toes accounted for...

But somehow, she still wasn't good enough.

Not good enough to keep, anyway. She was given away.

Abandoned.

Unwanted.

Not the bundle of joy most hope and can only pray for...

No, she was different.

A byproduct of fornication, the evidence of a love affair that didn't last...

The reflection of another that she would not come to know as her mother,

Although from her womb, she was birthed.

Being adopted just days after being in this world;

She began to grow and became well acquainted with the

Pressures of finding validation, acceptance, love, and the answers to questions she had in her mind,

But could not formulate into words...

PRESSURE...PAIN..PROMISE.

Her journey began...

A journey that would take her from the initial Pressures of life,

which caused much Pain,

yet, led her to The PROMISE.

A Journey that led from Darkness to her Destiny.

This is my story...

"For I know the thoughts that I think toward you, saith the LORD, thoughts of peace, and not of evil, to give you an expected end." Jeremiah 29:11

"Once upon a time..."

PRESSURE | CHAPTER 1

She was 8 years old when her daddy died. Too young to cry and way too young to understand, that never again would she see that old man that she loved more than life. And as the years tip toed by, she of course, grew older, and her body matured. Perhaps, too mature for a child because pretty soon, she was getting attention. Attention from men way too old to mention, just know they were way too old for her. Seeking the love one can only obtain from a father, she began to seek love in men who were much older. And at the tender age of 16, she became a mother. She said goodbye to innocence and embraced a stage in life she was surely not prepared for. But she stood there. Baby in one arm, books in another, and she continued to pursue. She stood there at the cross roads with a decision to make.

A decision to quit or pursue. A decision to retreat, or fight. A decision to believe or lose hope. A decision to live….or die. And she chose life. It's funny really. Because people look at her and think that she has it "altogether." As if every piece of her life is strategically and methodically perfectly positioned in its proper place. They have no idea how hard she fights daily – still to LIVE. A choice repeatedly must be made to live or die. A choice daily must be made to give up, give in and surrender or continue to fight like the victor she was created to be. Standing there at the crossroads, with tears in her eyes, pain in her heart, and shame on her face…she took a step forward, stumbling and in her mind, preparing to fall…until, He caught her.

> *"Before I formed thee in the belly I knew thee; and before thou camest forth out of the womb I sanctified thee, and I ordained thee a prophet unto the nations." – Jeremiah 1:5*

You see, her story wasn't over…it was just the beginning.

I don't remember the day I found out I was adopted. I think I always just knew something was "different". I didn't look like my mother. Not too much, anyway. Okay, not at all. It's as if, one day I just woke up and knew. No formal conversation or any tears or questions, I just one day knew. Perhaps that was enough. I remember my father, the only father I ever knew. He was gentle, kind, laughed a lot, and sometimes he was loud, – but he loved me more than life. He loved me like no one has ever loved me since.

But one day in 1981, he went into the hospital and never came home. I remember this vaguely because he didn't come to my sister's wedding later that year. We had family and neighbors over after the funeral as I later learned was custom, but I never cried. I never mourned. I never dealt with his death because I was too young to truly understand that I would never see him again. I could not comprehend that someone I saw daily was gone. Forever. Leaving my mother to care for me alone.

Honestly, growing up, I didn't realize my mother was a "single parent" until I became one. She continued to love me enough for both of them. Never missing a beat, she made sure I went to school and church – without excuses; and pushed me beyond limits - with her, there were none. I was in every sport and extracurricular activity I can remember and life went on…without my daddy. Yet, somehow I searched for him, well, the idea of him. The search went on for years. I searched for love in all the wrong places and in all the wrong people. I longed for the love only a daddy can give and as a result, I began to admire and adore older men. At first, it started with simple and casual conversation.

Young and naïve, I had no idea where idle conversation would lead. I just wanted the attention from a man. Someone who would replace the man that left without saying goodbye. An impossible mission for anyone but God. Yet I tried. And at the tender age of sixteen I became a mother. A stage in life I was surely not prepared for. No time to get ready and no written instructions on how to handle this – certainly no script provided with clear and concise details on how to tell your mother that her baby, is now having a baby. So, I didn't.

I hid it as long as I could. It was the month before my Sweet Sixteen birthday party, I will never forget. My sisters kept telling my mother that something was "wrong" with me. Implying consistently that I was pregnant, but of course, I denied it every time the question was asked. I wore big clothes anyway, as that was the style back then, so big shirts were never a cause for concern. So far, so good – my cover up was working. Although I slept a lot, I now believe that perhaps my mother and I were both in denial. Surely, the signs were there. However, one day the carefully played theatre production where I was the star of the show, came to a screeching halt. I was told that before any party could take place, I would have to go to the doctor for an exam.

My lie would be exposed and I had no other moves nor Plan Bs to protect my story line. So I went. And it was confirmed. I was eight months pregnant. Eight months of performing now over suddenly without warning and without a planned intermission to at least catch my breath. I had no words. No more lines. No more pretending. I was going to be a teenage mother at sixteen. Sweet Sixteen Party – CANCELLED.

After the initial shock of disappointment, embarrassment and anger wore off, my mother became overly protective. She made sure I ate tons and tons of vegetables. You must remember, eight months without any prenatal vitamins, we had a lot of catching up to do. This was our family's secret. No one else knew. I continued to play in the Symphonic and Marching Band in high school as well as sing in the church choir. Luckily we wore choir robes back then, so my little secret was well hidden. Until May 25, 1989, when my secret was revealed. A baby boy, my identical twin, we could have been siblings, but instead, he was my child. All of a sudden I was faced with an immediate decision. To fight and continue this journey or to quit and retreat. I wasn't raised to quit anything. I fought. I continued attending high school as usual. Other than missing only a few days to have my son, I didn't skip a beat. Tenth grade was not quite what I imagined.

My childhood dreams of becoming a lawyer – halted. How would I pursue my dreams now? I became the statistic I only read about. Single black teen-age mother, raised in a single parent home. Now what. There was a choice to make, and only I could make it. Many said after having a child at such a young age, that I would never finish school, let alone go to College and surely, never become an Attorney. I changed my role in the play of life and critics gave me no rave reviews. However, there was no other role I could audition for. This was the headliner – and I was the lead. My supporting cast, my mother. And she never allowed me to quit the show.

The next year, I switched schools. Now, a member on the dance/drill team and an active member in the chorus and several plays. The new beginning in a different environment gave me the fresh start I needed to no longer be "that girl" who had a child out of wedlock in the tenth grade. Honestly, I don't think may people ever knew. I believe that the stigma and shame placed on me, was put there by me. And it took many years to shake it away. Now, not only was I adopted, I was now a teenage mother. Alone. Faced with new adversities that I should not have known this soon. Unprepared to deal with a new born child and furthermore, ill prepared to deal with not only the physical change in my life, but the emotional and mental change as well. I began to suffer in silence, and no one knew. Not even me.

Oftentimes people suffer silently from undiagnosed diseases. Ashamed and afraid to get help – not truly knowing what they need or for what to specifically ask. Subtle thoughts of suicide became my headline for a story I was sick and tired of reading the lines for. The pain from the initial pressures of life began to enter without invitation and have a seat at the main table. An uninvited guest with no manners. Yielding its dark thoughts of ways to escape it all without saying goodbye. Suggesting ideas of suicide as my final curtain call with congratulatory flowers thrown over my grave and tears from friends and family as the applause.

PRESSURE...PAIN..PROMISE.

She Was Drowning, but No One Saw Her Struggle...

You may look at me and think I have it all together. But, behind my smile there's a pile of pain that slides down my face in the form of broken tears – whenever you're not around....

But when you ask me how I'm doing, I reply as if on perfect cue, "I'm Fine...",

when the Truth of the matter is that I'd rather forget the day began...No, not to try it again tomorrow, but to say my final goodbye to the repeated disdained disappointments to this very day that I did not want to see in the first place...

and I'm not even sure I WANT you to "Save Me" anyway...

Yes, my grin is fixed just perfectly.

I laugh with you during conversations and perhaps stay beyond my welcome because I know when I am "alone",

I have to deal with "Me."

I must face the reflection of rejection and smile anyway –

even if the grin hurts.

When I am with Me,

I must acknowledge the fact that I do NOT have it together as everyone perceives and erroneously believes –

and now, I criticize ME for not being better…

For not being further along on this journey than I am.

How did I get to this point?

I was depressed without proper diagnosis.

I cried just because.

Daily.

I stayed in bed for hours and hours, and days upon days,

far beyond the sun's rising….

Crying because I was ready to give up and die.

It would be easier – I thought.

Many days I fantasized about gracing the water with my chest….

taking my last breath…

I envisioned how my car would take its last dance on a carefully constructed bridge and be dipped into the arms of its lover –

PRESSURE...PAIN..PROMISE.

the sea,

its Mistress – Me,

as we are all intertwined in a

forbidden state of mind…

I even imagined driving my car dangerously yet somehow gracefully in excess of any regulated limit while closing my eyes

as if to lean in for a first Kiss…

Knowing he would not move before our touch –

the impact of the two now becoming one,

perhaps becoming many,

depending on how fast we

reached the crescendo together…

Yet, I passed the trees,

heart heavily racing as if I'm out of breath —

I thought about it…

A sudden swerve would be my "hello"…

I've

frequently

contemplated

Suicide.

PRESSURE | CHAPTER 2

It's difficult to seek help for a condition you are unaware of. The symptoms you dismiss as the result of long weary days. Hidden in your work and the affairs of others. Pleasing people and neglecting yourself. Every answer was yes, when inside you were screaming no. Yet, I kept extending myself. Continuing to seek that validation to know that you were in fact good enough. Longing to be desired to remove the brokenness of abandonment. Growing up in a loving home, with an abundance of "I love yous" received, still could not erase the pain that was engraved upon my heart and tattooed deep within my soul. As a result, I began to make irresponsible decisions, not understanding why. Not realizing that I was on a quest to quench a thirst that was impossible to satisfy.

Seeking a love I knew existed because I touched it once, I dated men repeatedly. In and out and in and out and in and out of relationships I went. Searching. Hoping. Longing for something I myself, was not ready to give nor was I prepared for. I wasn't whole. I wasn't ready. I was sick and did not know my prognosis. I was suffering. Silently. No one to turn to because it was my secret. College educated, raised in a good family home, surely I could not let anyone know that I was damaged. So I didn't. I continued on with life with my second secret that no one knew and I was determined to keep it that way. I graduated the following year, on time, with the rest of my classmates, with my secret in the audience watching. It must have been the need to start anew or perhaps just get away and escape the responsibility I was not yet prepared no equipped to handle, because after graduating high school, I enlisted into the United States Army. I attended the basic training as custom and once I was finally stationed in Fort Carson, Colorado, I sent for my son. We were on our own, nearly on the other side of the world away from my mother, but we managed. After my Honorable Discharge, nearly two years later, I was ready to come home and be a mother. It was time and the Army was not conducive for a single parent with a child. So, to Florida I returned.

Back home, finally in a place of familiar faces and an abundance of support, I was ready to pursue my dreams and my purpose. While in high school and during my brief stay in the Army, I was able to take college courses, so I had already begun my quest for something more. I attended college and worked full time as a correctional officer and began to care for my son, with my mother's unwavering help and assistance of course. Times were tough, but I was determined. In my last year of college, I became pregnant with my second child, my daughter. I met and fell in love with a man I knew would save me from my past. I believed again and thought, this was it. I was excited. This time, it wasn't a secret. Almost planned – I loved him, and this time, I thought we were ready. But the distance took a toll and eventually, the two year love affair, now evidenced by a new born child, began to experience some turbulence, but I held on tight to the bumpy ride. March 21, 1998, my daughter was born and May 1998, I graduated from Florida State University with my Bachelors of Science Degree.

And it's sad to say, less than a year later, distance and the lack of trust and solid foundation won. Again, I was a single parent. This time, I was shocked and in disbelief. I had failed hope and love was no longer my friend. It was time to tighten up those boot straps and fight. No time and certainly no permission to quit. So, we continued on – my two children and I. I remember one day, my daughter must have been perhaps 2 years old. I purchased my first home in 2000 and times were tough. I was living paycheck to paycheck at a job I didn't care for.

I remember coming home one afternoon after work after I picked my daughter up from daycare. We entered the house as usual, but this time, it was dark. Not the kind of evening that's planned with candlelight dinner or anything of the sort. This was an unplanned surprised evening of solace and solitude that I tried to revoke the invitation to.

No matter how hard I tried, the lights would not come on, no matter how many times I flipped the switch back and forth. That was it. That was the last straw. I finally broke. Completely. It was as if all of the pressures that I had successfully held in until now, were released without my permission. I fell on my bed, my head held up only by my hands so I could hide the tears. My child, Justice (who was named after my passion for the law), my angel, placed her small petite hand on my back and said to me, in a quiet, innocent yet authoritative voice, "Mommy, it's going to be okay." That's the day I got my second wind.

That day I learned first hand that children pay very close attention and watch you. They mimic your every word and oftentimes your every move. At that moment, although I was weak, she was my strength. So, at some point, perhaps I must have been strong. But that day, it's as if the roles were reversed and she was the guardian, comforting me. Encouraging me and telling me I couldn't give up because it was going to be okay. And it was, I made some arrangements after I "gathered myself" and the lights were turned back on later that night.

The pain was temporary, but the promise of my child telling me it was going to be okay, was permanent. And I must admit, both of my children, have constantly kept me when I felt as if I was going to give in. When the pressures began to feel almost unbearable, one of them would tell me it was going to be okay.. They declared and decreed the ending – that God would not forsake us, nor would He leave us. They assured me in their own childlike way, that the God who fed the fowls of the air, and the fish of the sea, was the same God who would provide for us. And He did.

They eased my pain with their love. It's as if they both have ALWAYS reassured me of it...Kinda like the way God always assures us that He loves us, in spite of our faults, failures and flaws. God never left, even when He probably should have. Even when we have left Him, over and over and over and over and over and over and over again, He still remains. Waiting for us to return to Him like the prodigal son. His arms opened wide and His love in tact. He is yet faithful in the midst of our unfaithfulness.

Luke 15:11-32 (NIV)

The Parable of the Lost Son

"There was a man who had two sons. The younger one said to his father, 'Father, give me my share of the estate.' So he divided his property between them. Not long after that, the younger son got together all he had, set off for a distant country and there squandered his wealth in wild living. After he had spent everything, there was a severe famine in that whole

country, and he began to be in need. So he went and hired himself out to a citizen of that country, who sent him to his fields to feed pigs. He longed to fill his stomach with the pods that the pigs were eating, but no one gave him anything.

When he came to his senses, he said, 'How many of my father's hired servants have food to spare, and here I am starving to death! I will set out and go back to my father and say to him: Father, I have sinned against heaven and against you. I am no longer worthy to be called your son; make me like one of your hired servants.' So he got up and went to his father.

But while he was still a long way off, his father saw him and was filled with compassion for him; he ran to his son, threw his arms around him and kissed him.

The son said to him, 'Father, I have sinned against heaven and against you. I am no longer worthy to be called your son. "But the father said to his servants, 'Quick! Bring the best robe and put it on him. Put a ring on his finger and sandals on his feet. Bring the fattened calf and kill it. Let's have a feast and celebrate. For this son of mine was dead and is alive again; he was lost and is found.' So they began to celebrate."

It's quite amazing how one can be preparing to celebrate,

while the other is still engulfed in pain.

PRESSURE...PAIN..PROMISE.

During this season of pressure, I thought the worst was, and that the future had to be better. I grieved, while I yet believed and all along, unbeknownst to me, God was preparing a feast. I suffered the thoughts of tomorrow when I should have only been concerned with the day at hand. The added pressures of life began to take their toil on my life. I wanted and yearned for more, but remained stagnant, allowing myself to become captured in the snares of enemy. Perhaps they, (the naysayers) were right all along. Maybe this was the best I would ever see. I began to doubt my dreams and aspirations and question what God originally said about my life. My childhood dreams of becoming an attorney were fading away – slowly.

I could not see the end of this journey being anything more than what it was at the moment. I was not satisfied with where I was, but could not see the way to get to where I wanted to be. The only constant in my life, was God. I began to seek him like never before. I began to see myself as the Prodigal son, and it was time for me to go back home. Back to the beginning where it all first began. For years, I placed the status of my identity in the hands of others. Seeking fancy titles and accolades that would show the world that I was somebody after all. I was on every Board of Directors you could imagine. Helping others, while I myself, was yet drowning. It was time to go back to the One who loved me first. The One who created me and fashioned me in His Image. It was time to surrender myself and my ideologies to the One who was the Alpha and the Omega, the beginning and the end. It was time to release the Pressure, because I could no longer bare the pain.

PRESSURE | 3

My sister girlfriend April, always told me, the best way to find out who YOU are, is to find out who GOD is – and when you get alone in His presence, that is when He will begin to speak to you and tell you who *you* are. I heard her for years, but I didn't immediately listen. I had grown accustomed to the thoughts and words of everyone else – and now, I was unsure if I could truly hear God's voice, and with all of my faults and failures, why would He take the time to speak to me. Besides, I had far too many voices in my head already that I allowed in… I was confused, unsure and full of self-doubt. I thought my story was over, until I got into His Presence.

In His presence, He began to speak to who I was and who I was destined to be. It was Sunday, May 14, 2000 – I was sitting in the back of the church, a familiar seat where I liked to "hide". And the preacher was preaching. He read from the following scripture:

Ephesians 1:5

> *"Paul, an apostle of Jesus Christ by the will of God, to the saints which are at Ephesus, and to the faithful in Christ Jesus: Grace be to you, and peace, from God our Father, and from the Lord Jesus Christ. Blessed be the God and*

Father of our Lord Jesus Christ, who hath blessed us with all spiritual blessings in heavenly places in Christ: According as he hath chosen us in him before the foundation of the world, that we should be holy and without blame before him in love: Having predestinated us unto the adoption of children by Jesus Christ to himself, according to the good pleasure of his will."

Wait a minute Lord, you mean I wasn't thrown away, unwanted or abandoned as I once believed…rather, I was CHOSEN? My life changed.

CHOSEN FOR A PURPOSE

She had a total of 5 babies. Three boys, two girls, but somehow, I was the one given away. Unwanted at birth, feeling thrown away, abandoned - or just maybe, I wasn't pretty enough. Was my cry too loud or was I the constant reminder of a love affair that shouldn't have been?

The byproduct of fornication - my biological father and I never met, all I've ever seen was a picture. For years, secretly inside I wept for the departure I didn't get the chance to say goodbye to. As a young girl, the man I knew and loved more than life whom I was blessed to call "daddy", died when I was merely 8 years old. So, growing up knowing I was adopted - on top of not having my daddy around - wondering how and why the woman that gave birth to me could just give me away - issues of abandonment became my headline..."What was wrong with me?" became an ever present melody in my head I honestly got tired of hearing - yet, it remained on repeat. Replaying the different scenarios that could have been or perhaps SHOULD have been...according to me.

But instead, my reality remained true - I was abandoned - given away, unwanted... As if, I was the defected one - not returned to sender, which I suspect could have been worse than being given up for adoption at birth. Somehow, the alternative still didn't make me feel better. Until one day I was sitting in church....it was a Sunday, May 14, 2000. The preacher was preaching about ADOPTION. He was talking about those being adopted by Christ, and how if you were adopted by Christ, that in essence you were CHOSEN. He went on to say that Christ looked at you and saw that in spite of your faults - in spite of the fact that your parents were drug addicts, or alcoholics, He wanted YOU. In spite of the fact that you may have come from a family full of issues - whatever that "issue" might have been, that He carefully selected YOU for a PURPOSE...

That the TRUTH of the matter is, you were NOT thrown away, but rather CHOSEN.

The rest of my story changed at that pivotal point in time. I came into my knowing and learned that MY TRUTH was that I was not thrown away as I once believed, but CHOSEN - and CHOSEN FOR A PURPOSE. Loved by a woman who did not have any birth children of her own - she PRAYED for me. She WANTED me. She SELECTED me as her own and loved me beyond words. What an honor it is to be CHOSEN.

After coming to myself, I began to believe again. I started to dream again. I remembered what God said years before concerning my life. I remembered the gifts he gave to me, and I started to write poetry again as I had done before – but now, it was therapeutic for my soul and necessary for my healing. I started to recall my passion – the law, and believed that if I was not thrown away, but rather chosen – then perhaps, what God said about me years before was indeed true. I was destined to pursue my dreams and passions again. I was renewed. I was refreshed. And I now, believed…I was born to do this.

YOU WERE BORN TO DO THIS!

Isn't it funny how a bird doesn't complain about the challenges it faces to learn how to fly…It's all they KNOW they are SUPPOSED to do…And that alone, is enough. The mere fact that they cannot immediately fly when they are born, does not discourage them – they somehow unapologetically just KNOW that they WILL when they CAN….

Similarly, YOU must KNOW with every ounce of your being that YOU were born with a PURPOSE….Destined to accomplish the task given to you by God….Created solely and distinctly to carry out the Gift given to you by your Creator….Yet, because you have not arrived YET, you have begun to question your ability….You've allowed the limitations of others' beliefs in themselves AND in you, to dictate what you KNOW you've been created to do.

But you've stopped pursuing based on a mere challenge…something designed to make you stronger… you've allowed it to paralyze you – you sit staring into nothingness, full of everything BUT hope and the desire you need to accomplish the task at hand…whether that task is to own your own business, or to write that book you've been talking about since Jesus left, or the test yet to re-take and pass…Maybe that song you've kept hidden, KNOWING it needs to be heard….

THAT IS WHAT YOU WERE BORN TO DO!

And you KNOW this….

But, the moment you REMEMBER this, you will step off of that limb called fear and immediately come to realize that you CAN FLY….

You just needed to spread your wings and let everything and everyone that's been weighing you down, fall OFF

(WHERE they fall, being the LEAST of your concern).

It's time to do what you KNOW you were BORN TO DO NOW.

PRESSURE...PAIN..PROMISE.

………..All I could say was YES.

Have you ever felt that there was more to life than what you were experiencing at the moment? As if to tell God, surely there is MORE to life than this? Barely living, just existing. Knowing there was more inside of you that you just had not tapped into. Everyone can see your purpose but you, yet you see the purpose and destiny in everyone else. Do you not believe that you too, deserve the promises of God? I didn't. But there was something down on the inside of me that I could not shake. It was as if God had placed a gift on the inside that I gracefully buried, but now, it was fighting to live. The gift knew it had a purpose.

Everyday without fail, there was a burning desire deep within me. It was a nudging in the late night hours and it would wake me up before the sun would rise. I could not let go of what God placed inside of me, no matter what the circumstances around me said. It did not look like success – surely it did not. It looked dark, hopeless… It looked like I would never be on top. It appeared that I would always be in lack and be the tail, never the head. But, I decided one day if God was amazing enough to place something inside of me that I could not let go of, something that when I wanted to give up and let it go, it would always pull and tug on me – I should be equally as amazing – created in His image, I decided to pursue my purpose. I applied to law school.

Yes, the teenage mother at the age of sixteen. The young girl who had low self-esteem and no knowledge of her true self, believed again.

One night I had a dream. In my dream, I saw the acceptance letter. It was dated on my birthday (April 28) – APRIL 28, 2004. I saw this as clear as day. I woke up excited because I expected God to fulfill His promise. The funny thing is – while others were waiting on me to fail – God had already spoken.

One thing I know about Him, is that He is not a man that He should lie. Everything that He speaks comes to pass. Never will His Word return to Him void. In fact, His Words are Yea and Amen. I received my letter of acceptance into FAMU College of Law the following day – it was dated, April 28, 2004. The Promises of God...

"For all the promises of God in him are yea, and in him Amen, unto the Glory of God by us." – 2 Corinthians 1:20 (KJV)

I thought that once I accepted the Promises of God, that all would be good. Right? It's like the misconception we all have, you know the one - that once you get saved, that all will be well and you will never experience any turbulence. That is not the truth….at all. In fact, if the devil is NOT busy in your life – if you *never* experience any trials in your life or any pressures whatsoever – there is grave cause for much concern. It's like the story of Job. Look at Job 1:8 (KJV), "And the LORD said unto Satan, Hast thou considered my servant Job, that there is none like him in the earth, a perfect and an upright man, one that feareth God, and escheweth evil?" Well, God apparently asked Satan if he considered me.

My first year of law school was one that was surely challenging. But I was excited about the opportunity. The first in my family to finish college and the first to attend law school. I was proud not just because I was accepted, but for what this meant for my mother and my children. I believed that now, all would be well. We would never have to struggle another day in our life. I planned that once I finished, I would remodel or build my mother a new house. My children would work if they wanted to, but not because they had to. Living would be easy. I already identified the vehicle I would purchase after I completed the course and knew in my soul, I would now be on top. My family and I would have issues to address – but finance was not going to be one of them. Until the house that I had purchased went into foreclosure. A solid blow to my spirit, the wind was knocked out of me. I was able to do a short sale at the last minute, and sold the home I could no longer afford. I was confused. I was on the track to assured success – but things were being taken away, and this wasn't the first.

PAIN | 4

One morning before work, while I was still living in Tallahassee, Florida at the time. My daughter and I was preparing for our day as usual. I was dressed and ready for work and getting ready to drop her off at daycare. I believe my son, Cameron (named after the father I never met) had stayed with his grandmother the night before. We walked out of the house – a brisk early morning...and my car was gone. I could not breathe from the pain, and was in disbelief although I knew what occurred. My daughter, as innocent as she was, proclaimed that someone "stole our car!" And I of course, agreed. I was blessed by God to have a home and a car – and now, the car was gone. So, when the foreclosure proceedings began, I thought to myself – again?

How long must I suffer while striving to provide for my family? How long must I endure things being taken away? First my car, now my home? Lord, you know I'm trying – but I remembered Job. In remembering his story – I recalled that he was not a foolish man and even when he was encouraged to, he never cursed God. So, I continued. First year of law school, done. Second year of law school, completed. Third year of law school....done. May 2007, I graduated from FAMU College of Law. The prior temporary pain didn't stop God's Plan, nor did the pressure abort the Promise concerning my life.

So many times, we allow the pressures of life to come in and take up more space than should be allowed. Then, we permit the pain to paralyze us and as a result, we remain stagnant. We no longer have the strength to pursue the dreams that used to keep us up and awake at night. We start to settle for "good enough" when we know God created us to be better.

Now that law school was over, I knew that my life had shifted. I knew that all the naysayers would be amazed in disbelief – that the little girl that was once abandoned, finally found her calling because her mindset changed. She was chosen now. She had a renewed sense of confidence that no one could shake. So I thought.

> **'The prior temporary pain didn't stop God's Plan,
> nor did the pressure
> abort the Promise concerning my life. '**

PRESSURE...PAIN..PROMISE.

WHEN SILENCE SCREAMS THE TRUTH

If I told you, you probably wouldn't be able to handle it. You see my smile, yet all the while, inside I'm hurting. But not the kind of hurt you can put a bandaid on and wait for it to heal...No, this kind of pain made me scream in silence.

An unimaginable and inaudible reaction to the truth of the matter. Ready to give up the ghost and die. The lack of tears would not permit me to cry. Head in the palm of my hands as I called His name – called his name desperately within my spirit – still, I could not speak. I dropped the phone and immediately, every ounce of hope that I carried the past 35 years came up and out....

Glad I didn't eat too much that day.

Hearing the news that the man I searched for and longed for, died...

Three months prior.

I never met my biological father...

And this haunted me for years.

Searching for a love only a Father could provide.

Failed relationships in search of validation –

an unqualified candidate doomed from day one.

Feelings of abandonment said hello to me daily...

An unwelcome conversation over Martinis –

but there was no Happy hour….

There were no giggles or outrageously loud sounds of laughter….

Only the presence of pain to keep me company…

I would rather be alone…

Alone in silence,

while inside my heart screams the Truth.

I foolishly thought that now with a Juris Doctorate Degree, that all of my prior pain had been clearly wiped away with no residue. It was another title right? It was further proof that I should not have been thrown away. Yet, I was still searching.

I contacted someone my sister saw on television who was a news anchor. She told me I should because he "looked like me" and he could possibly be my brother or relative at the very least. Well, when I finally heard from him – actually, his brother called. We talked casually. I explained to him as best as I could who my biological mother was and why I believed his uncle was in fact, my biological father. After a long uncomfortable pregnant pause - he (my cousin) told me that we found him – Cameron Zigfield Nurse, was his name.

Unfortunately, he passed away three months prior.... My voice shook as I screamed, "Noooooooooo!!!!" And the pain and hurt and disbelief came up and out. I dropped the telephone and ran to the restroom to vomit up the pain.

He was gone.

And I didn't get the chance to say Hello...

Or Goodbye.

Daddy...

For years I searched for you,

Knowing your name, but

Never knowing you, yet

I loved you just the same.

Gone without a proper goodbye

Or even hello,

No childhood memories to

Reminisce upon

No family portraits of you and my mother in love -

Just me.

Wondering for years if you remembered me, or

If I was a memory you wanted to forget.

But then you came to visit me, and

It was then I knew,

As you whispered loudly in my ear,

You loved me.

Although we never met. I longed for him. I searched for him and wanted to know if my features came from him. What did we have in common, if anything? Was our laughter the same and did we have the same quirky personality. But, all I had was a picture. I knew he loved music and played in a band. I also knew that he attended Florida State University – as did I to receive my undergraduate degree – perhaps that is one thing we shared. But, pictures and common likeness can never replace the emptiness you feel from never knowing your biological father. I think that had my father lived beyond the eight years we shared – then perhaps the void would have never been and I never would have searched for my biological father. But not having him, I still longed and I still searched – until the search was over.

What is important to know about pain is that it is temporary. That is why we are to never make permanent decisions in temporary situations or emotions. The word pain, has several meanings. One definition of pain is "physical suffering or discomfort caused by illness or injury…" Another, when used as a verb, defines pain as "to cause mental or physical pain to…", while it can also be defined as "careful effort; great care or trouble." Therefore, it is important to know that pain, while most times, is an uncomfortable disposition, it can also be a way of notifying you that something good is coming. The way a rainbow always follow the rain. Or the way a mother labors in great pain to give birth to her child, yet she knows assuredly without question, that once the pain is over, there is a good thing on its way. The crazy part about this example that is worthy to be noted, is that the mother never remembers the pain by itself..

The mother gives undivided attention and an abundance of focus to what was birthed *out* of the pain. In fact, if ever questioned, she will always assert that she would go through the process all over again because it was worth it. She somehow knows that every push through every ounce of pain and suffering, is worth the promise that was delivered.

Romans 8:18 describes it best:

"For I reckon that the sufferings of this present time are not worthy to be compared with the glory which shall be revealed in us."

PRESSURE...PAIN..PROMISE.

PAIN | 5

WIPE YOUR EYES, IT'S NOT WHAT IT LOOKS LIKE

Many of us are/were in what we THOUGHT was a "PIT" place – you know, a place that is surely NOT where WE PLANNED nor DESIRED TO BE!!!

BUT, if you DUST OFF what the carnal eyes see...

if you take the time to cast away your Doubt and Unbelief...

to put aside any Selfishness, YOUR DESIRE and IDEOLOGIES of what YOU THINK OUGHT TO BE and WHEN it ought to be, and COMPLETELY TRUST GOD and

HIS PLAN for your life,

THEN you will come to find that you're REALLY in the PALACE – Placed there to BE A BLESSING to someone ELSE!

What may be "uncomfortable" to YOU,

MAY be the ANSWER to someone else's PRAYERS!!!

Be ye therefore CAREFUL in "cursing" where you are RIGHT NOW....

For in DUE SEASON,

the DUST SHALL BE WIPED AWAY

and what you THOUGHT was a DARK PLACE,

you will find was REALLY A SET UP TO BLESS YOU!!!!!

So, wipe your eyes, it's NOT WHAT IT LOOKS LIKE!

STOP FOCUSING ON THE PAIN...

AND FOCUS ON THE PROMISE.

I don't know who told the story that no one can ever miss what they never had. I missed my biological father even though we never met. I missed the man who raised me until I was eight years old and my memories of him were few. So, let me tell you that you can in fact miss something you have never experienced before. You possess a longing and a desire to experience something you've only imagined. You know in your knowing that it belongs to you – but it is missing – for whatever reason. Perhaps you were adopted or raised in a single parent home. Maybe your father or mother passed away while you were yet at an early age. Whatever the situation, you longed for their presence…Needing closure you never imagined would come. Until one day, it is there.

For whatever reason, God has always spoken to me through my dreams. It was when I was finally still and away from the pressures and interruptions of the day that He would speak clearly like never before. I am sure He spoke while I was awake as well, I just didn't always take the time to be still enough to hear and listen to him. So at night, sometimes He would send visions or messages to me in my dreams. It was strange, unfamiliar but I was not afraid. I welcomed the opportunity to hear from my Father.

This particular night I was asleep, God thought enough of me to send closure. Although I was asleep, it was as if I was ever present and well aware. In the far corner of my bedroom, I saw a man that looked like me. His skin was fair and his hair a dark brown, almost black. I moved slowly towards him and I knew immediately who he was. My biological father, I remembered him from the picture. But, my in my dream, he was much older than the man I saw in the picture years ago.

He embraced me and it was better than I ever dared to imagine. He held me tight and whispered in my ear and I heard him loudly, "I love you." At that moment, every part of my being was thankful. I can't explain it, but the hug appeared to have lasted forever – perhaps we were on Heaven's time. I woke up with a flood of tears in my eyes. He came to say goodbye to his baby girl.

Shortly after graduation from law school, my mother said it was time to come home. After receiving my degree and having not found employment in the Orlando area immediately there afterwards, I returned home to accept employment. There I worked and traveled quite extensively. Still, it didn't seem enough. I didn't know at the time what it was, but I did not feel fulfilled. It was as if I knew there was something else out there for me to do. My passion was calling me daily but I refused to answer. Not knowing how to begin to pursue, I placed it on the back burner. I worked for two other employers and even began working with a network marketing company. There, I began to find my way. I began to step out on faith – perhaps too soon as others believed, but I stepped out anyway. I said good bye to the corporate world and hello to my passion for the first time. A nervous hello, I might add. But we met, nonetheless.

For nearly two years, I traveled and worked hard in the networking company while trying to build my unemployment appeals consulting company simultaneously. I had my hands in everything and was everywhere – a jack of all trades, but a master of none. I did not understand that what I was doing was searching. It just looked different – a distinction without a difference. I was longing for something to fulfill this emptiness I had inside that I did not know existed or at least, I pretended not to know. On the outside, everything looked as if it was well put together. Friends would send personal messages via social media saying how well I was doing and how I was obviously doing "very well" for myself. They had no idea. On the outside, I looked great – hair and nails done, BMW clean as a whistle – sometimes I would take my last and make sure I at least "looked the part". I was desperately pleasing people that only knew my name, but had no insight to my story. I was concerned with the thoughts of others, yet took no true and honest thought for myself. I was trying to get to know everyone else and meet their needs, while my needs went lacking. I would take my last and bless someone else – when I myself, was in need. Some would say, "aweee, that's nice, you're a giver." While that may be true, you cannot afford to save others, while you, yourself, are drowning. I learned from a friend, who is appropriately known as Mastermind, not too long ago and it yields to be true today, "You must participate in your own rescue." This resonated with me and I remembered it often whenever I would feel overwhelmed from the pressures and pain of life.

After research, I found a story that tells of a student who shared a narrative that bought a visual understanding of the profound statement he shared. A friend of hers was on a whitewater rafting trip in Colorado. During the trip, one of the people in the raft fell out into the river. He floundered around passively while the guide attempted to steer the raft towards him. The guide offered assistance but the man remained passive. Finally, the frustrated guide shouted, "Participate in your own rescue!"

There is a key lesson in this story. Life is suffused with senseless, self-inflicted, stress, misery, dissatisfaction, and suffering. However, many of us sit there complaining about our situation and never do anything about it. Yelling out for help from others when oftentimes, we are well equipped to rescue ourselves. This was my story. The reason why I, and so many others haven't saved ourselves is because we aren't frustrated enough to even think of participating in our own rescue!

It is important to know however, that when you begin to participate in your own rescue, it will not feel good. The waves will appear to overtake you, fear will begin to set in, but you must remain calm in the midst of the fight. Yes, even when the fight is with yourself.

After I stepped out on faith, I erroneously thought that God would make every way smooth and the turbulent waves would come to a sudden calm. The story of Job was a faint memory, I thought my story would be different.

I believed.

I was ready to pursue.

I stepped out.

All was supposed to be well now.

Because I lost my home nearly to foreclosure, I had to get an apartment once I returned back home. This particular year, one year after I leaped, I received the notice that no one wants to see. The Three-Day notice. I was on my way to Kentucky for a convention and thought all would be taken care of. If you ever want to have a humbling experience, have your child come home from school and walk up to her apartment home to find her belongings along with the rest of your household items outside thrown inside of garbage bags in the parking lot as if it was yesterday's trash. Then, because you aren't there, your mother and son have to pick all of the items up and plea with the management to allow you to put your items back into the apartment until you return to town. Talk about a humbling moment.

Walking among thousands of people, millionaires and the like, smiling and pretending that everything was okay, when on the inside I was screaming for help. No one knew. Everything was falling apart but I was trying to hold it together. Thankfully, we were able to stay until the end of the month – May 6 was the end of my lease, but because I was unable to renew, I was permitted to stay until the end of the month. I borrowed the money to pay the outstanding balance I owed and when I returned home, began to look for someplace else to live. I apologized to my family for the eviction – they never should have taken part in such a thing. My mother never had our things put out in the street, and I never wanted this for my children. It was a scene I wish I could delete – but I couldn't.

I thought moving would be easy. I was always able to rebound one way or another, but this time it was different. No doors opened, and I was stuck. Two weeks, I said. That's all I needed and everything would be okay again. A friend helped me pack up the apartment – a lot of valuable items with sentimental value were broken, so the heartbreak was renewed as we began to sort through items that I could keep and those things that I would need to throw away. The progress began, but I did not know exactly where I was going. The plan was no longer mine, and I was no longer in control.

Thank God for mama. I returned home, and found a place on her couch. Technically, you could say I was homeless. My mother's home was a three bedroom and one bath home, approximately a little over 1400 square feet. Now, there lived my mother, my son, my daughter and me. My daughter slept in my old room, not how I imagined life at 41 years old. I felt like a failure. Unable to sleep at night and throughout the day, I lived at Starbucks and did my unemployment appeals work there from my laptop. I packed clothes in my trunk with personal items just in case a friend was kind enough to let me crash with them. My mind was incapable of being focused and my search now, was intensified. A dear friend whom I've known since I was twelve, told me something was wrong. I was different. Not quite the same. Perhaps others noticed but were too afraid to speak and tell the truth. It was strongly suggested that I speak with a Doctor and just tell him what was going on. Reluctantly I did and that's when I was finally diagnosed with Depression and Anxiety. Finally. The panic attacks had a name. Before, I just knew I would cry and couldn't breathe.

Still, I was dissatisfied with where I was, and I believed that surely, this was not a part of God's plan, but the play had to continue. The next scene was coming up with no intermission and I had to continue playing the role of the one who had it altogether. I continued to attend social functions, oftentimes borrowing money for gas. I continued to attend church when it took everything in me to just get there. Sometimes, I would have just enough gas to get there and get home – but I knew that was my safe house and I did not have to pretend anymore. I could cry and no one would judge me. I could stay on my knees as long as necessary and someone would be there to help me up. There, on the Altar, I could release it all – the pounding pressure and all of the pain. I lost myself in Him, and there, I finally found Myself.

She Left it at the Altar...

She was broken,

pretending to be whole.

But this day, she was finally tired.

Tired of being tired.

Exhausted from the run of hiding – afraid of the commitment because she did not believe she was strong enough.

She didn't want to disappoint her Father again...

She was tired of letting Him down –

so she ran from His presence and His Glory.

She escaped accountability and buried her gifts and talents

because inside she knew...

She knew that once she completely surrendered,

there would be a new level of responsibility and

she would not be able to

PRESSURE...PAIN..PROMISE.

turn back and hide anymore....

But this day, at the Altar,

God snatched her up and the chains of bondage were broken.
Every lie that the enemy ever told was destroyed and

God's Word saturated her spirit, her soul,

the very essence of her being.

In the midst of His Presence,

She finally surrendered it all –

her body...

her mind..

her emotions,

her past,

her pain...

all of the pressure,

she left it at the Altar.

She was NEW. She was HEALED..She was FORGIVEN...

She was finally made WHOLE.

41 years old. Sleeping on my mama's couch, with a Juris Doctorate degree...driving a BMW. The familiar song began to play again, "What is wrong with me?" Some days, if I had enough money, I would get a hotel room for the night just to have some sense of normalcy. I smiled my way trough the pain and no one knew the truth, but a select few. Why was I here? "Why," echoed to God and surely, He must have grown tired of my cry.

One afternoon, I was sitting in the waiting room at the Eye Doctors' office. A lady sitting next to me asked if I was "Jackie's child". Confused as to how this lady knew me and was bold enough to ask me about a woman that did not raise me. I responded, "No, I am not. I am Lucille Hawkins' child, but, Jackie is my biological mother." Honestly, I could understand her inquiry. My biological mother and I look nearly identical. Nevertheless, after the clarification was made, the lady went on to say how my mother always had children around her because she said when she grew old, she did not want to be alone. Fighting back the tears, my answer came in the form of a borderline rude answer, from a mere stranger.

Later that week, as if God needed to send a confirmation. My mother told me the story of how she prayed to God that when she got older, she never wanted to be alone. I knew then, every set back, most of my doing when I moved without consulting God for direction, was all apart of God's divine plan. I was where I was supposed to be. So, it is in life.

Oftentimes we are in a place that we believe is the pit. It feels like the lowest place we could ever be. It is uncomfortable, and if I may be real – it hurts. It can be embarrassing and make you doubt not only yourself, but every promise that God ever spoke over your life. You will even begin to think that maybe you never heard from God at all. Not realizing that where you are, in actuality, is the palace. You just need to open your eyes and see clearly – you need to dust off the current circumstances of a temporary situation.

PAIN | 6

She prayed for me…

And here I am,

trying to leave the Palace and abort her blessing -

…Not knowing, I was the sacrifice.

I began to wonder, okay, God, here I am – what's next? How can I rebuild what has been drastically torn down? This fall was pretty steep, and I was unsure of how to climb out of the hole. I had a car I could not afford to pay for. I was sleeping on my mother's couch, and renting hotel rooms or staying with friends one to two nights at a time, to not out stay my welcome. It was as if everything I believed I should have, was taken away. This was a pivotal time in my life. Yet, there was something in me that would not give in.

I cannot lie to you. This one hurt. Badly. Every time before, I was able to rebound rather quickly, with little to no residue. Surely not enough evidence to show where I had been. But, this was different. I did not hold a sign on a street corner. I did not sleep in a shelter, but let me be transparent - I was homeless. A suitcase filled with clothes and papers pertaining to the telephonic unemployment hearings I held from my car. Whether I was at a lake, or parked in a parking lot somewhere, I would have my papers and notes spread about the front seat. They had no clue. Friends would see my trunk and jokingly ask, "Girl, what are you doing!? Living out of your trunk?" They had no idea how true their statement was. Jokingly, I would always reply, "Yes!!!!" Followed by an ounce of laughter, but I was being honest.

At one point, I leased an office to conduct my business affairs. Remember, I had an image to uphold. Not just the image, but it grew to be a burden trying to hold hearings inside of my car. Extremely hard to be organized if you can imagine. At that time, I had a friend who believed in me and supported my dream, and loaned me the $600 I needed to get started in the office. God always seemed to place angels around me who would support me exactly where I was. That's why it's important to know who is in your circle. People around you should be able to do two very important things: Tell you the truth, and support you. If you have a group of people around you that do neither, it's time to change who you're hanging around.

Fanfare is lovely, but someone who will push you towards your purpose, even when you feel like throwing in the towel; now, that's a beauty to behold.

I could not believe it most days. I had an office, but did not have a home to call my own. I had an assistant that I could barely afford to pay. It was an experience of transition and change I surely did not sign up for. Yet, I was in it.

Have you ever been in a place where you knew you did not belong? Have you ever seen yourself in a place or position of greater? I mean, actually *saw* yourself? The very thought of

PRESSURE...PAIN..PROMISE.

something better ought to frustrate you to the point that you begin to push beyond the pain and push beyond your breaking point and know that in the midst of it all, God is making you.

YOUR BREAKING POINT IS YOUR MAKING POINT

It hurts.

It's uncomfortable.

Perhaps even unfair and most certainly, undeserving.

Yet, it is nonetheless, NECESSARY.

With the constant pain you feel from the daily pressures of life,

"Why?" becomes the question of the hour and

without an answer,

your frustration only becomes heightened and

you begin to question yourself –

So much to the point of even questioning your Purpose.

But here's something you MUST remember –

everything you are experiencing right now is connected to your destiny and essentially a part of your journey to your Promise.

But, the KEY to unlocking the manifestation of God's promises in your life is to not fall apart during the process of the "BREAKING", yet instead, to "gather yourself" and turn your "Breaking Point" into your "MAKING" point..

You need to know that this is NOT how your story will end. This is just the beginning...

You won't die here.

You won't fall apart.

You won't lose your mind.

You won't fail.

You ARE destined to WIN – if you faint not.

I believe that's really the key to enduring pain, to not give in and faint. Although it hurts, and surely is uncomfortable, you must never surrender to pain. Pain is like an ex-lover who can never come back because your heart has endured too much damage and its presence alone, while familiar, makes your heart sick and your soul grieve. It's what you do with and how you handle the pain that will determine the rest of your journey and the end of your story.

"Will you allow PAIN

to CONSUME you

or

FUEL you?"

Whenever you get tired and feel like giving up on your dreams – let your PASSION PUSH you through the PAIN....Only then, will you reach your PROMISE. Here's what you need to know. Since the very day you were born, God purposed and designed destiny for your life. The key to finding your way in this life, is no secret. In fact, it lies in knowing Him. Seeking validation and approval in anyone other than the Lord the Most High will always prove to be fatal. But, seeking to please Him, even when you fall, as you sometimes will – will bring about change and assured transformation. But, how to do you fight through the pain during the process of change?

HOW TO GET BEYOND THE **PAIN**

1. **Help others even when you are in need.** This will make you appreciate exactly where you are and in helping others, it makes you feel better. Zig Ziglar said it best when he stated: *"You can have everything in life you want if you will just help enough other people get what they want."*

2. **Don't complain while you're helping.** We are quick to pray to God and ask Him to bless us, so that we can be a blessing. However, oftentimes, while we are blessing others, it may interfere with our regularly scheduled day. It may feel as if it is completely inconvenient. During our "helping" we constantly complain. And we miss it. If you truly want God to use you, He will use you according to their (whoever He intends to bless) needs – not when it's most convenient to you. When you're truly blessing someone – it's not about you.

3. **Don't look at the Needle.** I remember whenever I needed to have blood drawn, I was always afraid to look at the needle. But, when I set my mind upon something else – whether it was on what I had to do

later that day, or just idle conversation for the moment, it was over before I knew it. Therefore, keep your focus on the promise, not the pain.

4. **Pain is not Permanent.** When you're going through the pain, it will feel as if it will last forever and there is no way out. Know that pain is not permanent unless YOU choose to stay there. Remind yourself what God said about your life and hold tight to His Word and continue to fight.

5. **Let God BE God and Trust Him through the Pain.** The way to get to your Promise, is to TRUST God through your pain. Know that the Pressure, and even the Pain is necessary to get to the Promise.

PRESSURE...PAIN..PROMISE.

This is just the Process, not the Goal

Don't fall so in love with the "PROCESS" that your "PROCESS" becomes the "GOAL". The process, (i.e, the journey or what you are going through right now) is NOT THE GOAL!

The "Process" is simply a collection of experiences and lessons – THE GOAL is the GOAL!

It's your Expectation of what God said He would do and the manifestation thereof!

Be cautious as to Not get caught up and STUCK where you are!

Get FOCUSED and MOVE FORWARD!

You've been in the "Wilderness" LONG ENOUGH....

Your 40 years of just "walking around" is OVER!

It's NOW TIME for you to walk into your Promise!

How do you walk into your promise?

You must STOP FOLLOWING, and START LEADING!

Are you Ready?

Then Declare it then!

Where I am NOW is NOT where I am destined to BE!

It's time to MOVE!

You haven't been through ALL that you've been through just to glorify and remain in the process! It's time for you to get to the Promise Land and enjoy the manifestations of God!

But, YOU GOTTA MOVE!!!!!!

PROMISE | 7

There's something to be said about the person who just won't quit. When it seems as if all hope is lost and there is no where else to turn. When you have done all that you can, but you still remain in the same place. You stand there strong in the Lord, and you let Him be your strength. Be not confused about the process, it will not be easy, but it will be worth it. By the age of 42, I had lost my first home, I had three vehicles repossessed, I filed bankruptcy in hopes of a new and better beginning, only to repeat the same financial mistakes. I was now the single parent of two children and I was tired. Yet, I began to tithe like never before because I knew the little money I did have, was not and would never enough.

For two years I was without corporate employment and a steady paycheck. Not one day went by where I was without food or shelter. Not one day came when my children did not have food to eat or proper clothes to wear. My daughter participated in every event there was at her high school and traveled with the theatre group she was actively apart of. Even while sleeping on my mother's couch, God still provided. He exceeded my expectations in the midst of my frustration from the pain.

During this process, my mind and the way I was thinking began to shift. In the latter part of 2015, my Pastor began a series entitled, "Go Get Your Life." This was the paradigm shift for me as that was the moment I truly began to believe again. He preached several subjects that completely aligned with where I was at the moment. It was as if God told him my most intimate and sacred secrets and he knew all about me, my disappointments and my failures. I tried to hide in church, so he could not see me exactly where I was. I was ashamed of the failures I encountered so far in this life. So, I sat on the far right side of the church, out of the way, and out of view – so I thought.

However, when there's a call on your life and God has a work for you to do, you cannot run and hide forever. He will pick you out of the crowd to do His Will. You only must be willing. I was far from perfect. In no way did I have it together, but God decided to use me in spite of me, and I was truly honored.

When there's a work for you to do in the Kingdom, your past matters, but not in the way you would think. Actually, it is your past that has prepared you for such a time as this. If you have never experienced heartache, you can't talk to me about my heart being broken. If you've never failed a bar exam, you can't talk to me about having the will to try again and encourage me to not throw in the towel and just quit. If you've never been depressed and sick of yourself, you can't talk to me about picking myself up and getting out of bed, because you've never been there so you don't know nor can you imagine what it feels like. If you've never been adopted and felt abandoned, you're surely not qualified to tell me how to overcome my abandonment and trust issues and just get it together...And most assuredly, If you've never bore pain, you can't tell me how much it hurts because you've never felt it. But, if you've been through something and God brought you out – you can tell me about hope, and I might believe again.

Going through the various series topics at my church, which included: "Shift", "Go Get Your Life", and "I Still Believe", I started to believe again and I had a glimpse of hope. My language began to change. I started to believe that if God wanted to, He would – and if for whatever reason, He didn't – it wasn't because he couldn't, but rather because He had something better. In the midst of going through the pressures and pain of this life, you have to completely trust Him in all that you do. The same is true even in relationships. Before, I used to think if someone left or if a relationship didn't work out, it was because something was wrong with me. I would even ask, "what did I do?" And sadly to say, I would try to make it better so they would stay. But the greatest gift you could ever give yourself is the right to say "goodbye." I started to realize that there was nothing wrong with me. I was a diamond in the making. If someone didn't want to be with me it was because God didn't trust them with His most precious jewel and as a result, now my rebound time from the heart break was quick and without apology. I was ready for what God had for me and I refused to settle for anything else.

I remember when I used to pray to God that He would send me someone to lean on and help me through whatever it was I was going through. I was tired of going through it alone. Of course, I asked for other things as well – but my intent and my motive wasn't right, neither was my heart completely healed. I wanted a relationship with a man more than I wanted a relationship with God. I wanted someone to fill the emptiness and void I still felt because I was given away.

God knew it, but I was in denial. He knew He couldn't trust me. But there came a point in my life where I said, "God if you don't bring anybody else, I'll be satisfied with loving You." I had poured everything I was into Him and understood that all that I needed, *He* would provide – not a man.

During this shift, I began to long for God's presence throughout the day. I would work on my blog that I started after people kept encouraging me to write a blog in lieu of ridiculously long status posts on social media, and find myself in worship. I would be driving and have to pull over because I thought of the goodness of Him alone. I began to search God like never before. I got naked before Him and finally told the truth – confessed to what He all along knew.

For the first time in my life, I was no longer playing a role of who I wanted to be. There were no fancy well written lines to recite and no wardrobe changes; it was just me and God, and I was uncovered. I was vulnerable like I have never been before, and it felt uncomfortable. I laid down my failed plans of what I thought should be and my ill mannered ideologies and trusted God completely.

Before I knew it, things began to change. I began taking the antidepressants less often because now my passion kept me awake at night and thoughts of my promise and purpose, woke me up in the mornings. I didn't want to go to sleep and forget the day anymore, I wanted to know what God was saying concerning my life. I began to think of creative ways to dig myself out of the financial hole I was in and so I began to participate in my own rescue....

...And God moved.

PROMISE | 8

The BMW that I would have to peak around the corner as I opened the door to begin my day, and hope and pray would still be there, was now paid for - in full. The very thing that not one month prior, I was unsure if I would be able to keep, I now held the clear title for, with no liens attached. And because I think God just wanted to show off, the payoff amount was $10,000 *less* that the total amount I owed! But God didn't stop there. My mother and I began to discuss plans to enclose the car porch to give me some type of privacy. We planned to add a room so I can move from the sofa to my own bed. Talks of enclosing the car porch turned to completely remodeling the home and building it to our specifications with me, the chief designer and the home now in my name. I didn't have any money and my credit was despair. I was unsure how I would ever be able to afford or be in position to buy another home. But, here we were, building a Palace from the ground up, debt free. The three bedroom and one bath home would now be a four bedroom, one office, and three bath home. Talk about double for your trouble!

Nearly 3,000 square feet of a new home was underway not because of anything special that I did, but simply because the pit was never the pit – it was the palace all along, it just needed to be transformed into its proper state. It needed to be transformed into what God had purposed for it to be all along. That's why I kept coming home, because that's where I was meant to be. Imagine if I had moved again under my own direction, without consulting God, in a hurry to "get away" and follow the "norm" of the crowd. What if I had continued to be concerned with what others thought about a now, 42 year old living at home with her mother. I would have missed it completely. My mother says to this day that I was her blessing. I must respectfully disagree. My mother saved my life when she chose me to love as her own and saved me from myself.

It is important to know that your promise is birthed out of your pain. That is why we cannot run from it, but go through it. If you attempt to go around the pain and the pressures of life, you will without question or doubt, abort your promise. Each one of us has a gift that God has placed inside of us. However, we get so busy with the daily demands of life and those around us, that we aren't still enough to hear him and certainly do not take the time to listen. Once I stopped running, my gifts began to make room for me.

It was a Sunday morning, during church service. I had just returned from a workshop in Atlanta and learned insightful tips and instructions on how to write a book and publish it in 30 days. The day before I attended the event, I started a blog. I had no clue how to write a book – wanted to, but the fear and not knowing how to actually get started, held me captive to the idea and I never manifested the dream before. While at service this particular morning, my Pastor called me out, in the middle of his message, and told me that I had books to write and that those I was around, while I admired them, that I was just as talented, if not more. This blew my mind and made my baby jump. I was pushed into my purpose because someone saw something in me that I did not see myself or if I may be honest, saw, but pretended not to see, because of fear.

Fear will paralyze you if you let it. Being afraid and stuck in your emotions will always keep you right where you are. I'm sure you've heard of the saying about insanity. The definition of insanity is doing the same thing over and over again, while expecting a different result. I'd like to add, insanity is also listening to those who want to keep you where you are. That's why it's important to know who you're around and to be cautious of who you're listening to. You should be mindful of who you are following and who you are allowing to speak into your destiny. Not everyone should be allowed to go with you on your on your journey. Most will cause you to carry weight you can not afford to carry and as a result the journey will take much longer, if you reach your destination at all. Therefore, be mindful of who you allow to stand in your intimate circle, and be equally as strategic in who *you* are around. To be successful, you must get around successful people. Find those who have been where you want to go. Keep in mind, you must be willing to do what successful people do, and that will require a sacrifice.

A sacrifice can be anything from giving up watching television, or hanging out with your friends when you, instead, should be working on your craft or your gift. You, could be the sacrifice. Are you willing to lay down your life so that others might live and be free? I don't mean lay down your life literally, but rather – figuratively. Are you willing to tell someone how you contemplated suicide but your faith in God saved you. Are you willing to get naked before the people if you knew it would save someone else from experiencing the same hurts you endured? Are you willing to tell your personal story of truth – even if your voice shakes?

If you choose to help others and walk in your purpose, you must be willing to do the very thing you fear the most. For me, it was sharing my story. I told it to friends on many occasions without giving any thought of it at all. But I realized that there were others out there who were going through the same pain I once experienced and was still experiencing, and they needed to hear my story. Their life depended on it. I was never a public speaker, but I needed to nonetheless share my story, even if my voice shook. And it did.

My first paid speaking engagement was at my church. It was very brief, but I was nervous. It would be the first time I would be open and completely vulnerable in front of a group of people. I remember saying how I never thought I would speak in front of people and a lady looked at me in great disbelief. I learned that day the very thing you may be afraid to do, is perhaps what God has called you to do. When you have an understanding that it's God's calling on your life and not you, yourself, you are able to walk in authority in the thing that once brought about fear, but, now brings about faith.

What have you been afraid to do? Don't you think it's time for you to do it? What are you afraid of? How long will you allow fear to hold you captive to your dreams and your goals? Today seems like a good day to hit "Reset" and start again.

The awesome thing about telling your story is that while it is designed to help others, it ends up blessing you the more you tell it. There's healing in your story when you continue to tell it. In fact, the more you tell it, the more you grow as a person. Each time you will remember a moment where you know it was no one but God that brought you out. And the story that once brought you tears to tell, now brings joy and laughter because you realize as you're standing there, you didn't die in it. Whatever your story is, it's time to tell it. People are depending on you to be delivered from their pain and they are waiting on you. Stop saying you aren't qualified or gifted or talented enough. You just need to tell it. Now.

It doesn't matter at all what you've done, where you've been or where you came from - if you were adopted, or perhaps grew up in a single parent home. It doesn't matter how many times you fell down, if you but only continue to believe. You must know in your knowing that the pain didn't and won't break you. All along I erroneously believed that because I was given away, my life would never be what God intended it to be. On the contrary, my life was exactly as God planned.

In Isaiah 55:8 it reads:

> "For my thoughts are not your thoughts, neither are your ways my ways, saith the LORD. For as the heavens are

higher than the earth, so are my ways higher than your ways, and my thoughts than your thoughts. For as the rain cometh down, and the snow from heaven, and returneth not thither, but watereth the earth, and maketh it bring forth and bud, that it may give seed to the sower, and bread to the eater: So shall my word be that goeth forth out of my mouth: it shall not return unto me void, but it shall accomplish that which I please, and it shall prosper in the thing whereto I sent it."

PROMISE | 9

Your Greater is coming because you didn't quit...

I wanted to surrender,

But I couldn't.

There were days I did not know how I made it through, and

Certainly thought that I wouldn't -

But, here I am.

The pressures of life tried to overtake me

And the pain attempted to forsake me,

But the promises of God made me

Into who I am today.

That's why you, cannot quit

There's too much inside of you, therefore,

You must fight like your life depends on it,

Because it does.

You were created to do this

Everything you've been through -

PRESSURE...PAIN..PROMISE.

Prepared you for this.

How dare you say you're ill equipped, just because

You're full of fear

With no faith in sight.

But this is your time,

Your kairos

To make the wrong things right.

What the devil meant for evil

God is using it for your good -

Don't try to understand the process

It will never be understood.

Our ways are not His ways,

Our thoughts, surely not His thoughts -

But the process is defining who you were destined to be,

And the pain from all of the pressure,

Is not for naught.

When questions remain, "why didn't she want me", or "was I not good enough?", you must trust in God's infinite wisdom and knowing that regardless of how you feel while going through the process, it is all working for your good.

Romans 8:28

"And we know that all things work together for good to them that love God, to them who are the called according to his purpose."

In Him, I found all of the answers to the questions I had in my heart but could never formulate before. It wasn't that my biological mother did not want me, but rather, a lady who could not have children of her own, prayed for me. She chose me. God had to remove me from where I was because He had to answer a fervent prayer from a woman who loved Him more than herself.

So many times we think that we are a victim in a situation, when the truth of the matter is, that we are not only the *victor*, but we are an answered prayer – a *blessing*. Stop thinking that you are less than who God created you to be. He has a divine appointment and purpose for your life. He created you for such a time as this and everything that He destined in your life, has to come to pass, because He already said that His Word would not return to Him void. But you, have to stop running. Stop running away from your purpose and your destiny just because it is unfamiliar and feels a bit uncomfortable. Get out of yourself and get into Him and there, you will find your purpose and your promise.

The moment I accepted God's divine purpose for my life, that's when things began to change. I looked and felt differently. I knew that it was no longer about me, rather, it was about His plan for my life. That, I believe, is the key to finding out your purpose, to know and accept the fact, that it is not all about you. When you are being used by Him, you must surrender your thoughts and agendas and be willing to be used by Him, even if there are no titles given.

The moment you "pause" and decide to truly search God and find yourself, people will leave, but that's okay. One thing you need to know is that while you are in pursuit, you have to be so focused on finding your purpose, that if all of your friends leave you and you suddenly realize, no one is there, you must be willing to stand even if you have to stand alone and pursue God for yourself by yourself.

When you are finding your purpose and in pursuit of God's promise, here are a few tips to remember:

1. It's not about you.
2. Your Pain is connected to your Promise, so embrace it, don't try to erase it.
3. Stay focused on what God said, paying no attention to your present circumstances.
4. Build a relationship with God, and then with yourself.
5. Spend time alone, fall in love with you, only then can you love anyone else.
6. Your gifts will make room for you, therefore, you can turn your passion into profit once you've identified your purpose.
7. You will get knocked down, but you can get back up.
8. God is able – even if He doesn't do something, it's not that He can't, He just has something better for you.
9. Everything is done in God's timing, not yours, so do not get weary in well doing, for in due season, you shall reap, IF you faint not.

10. DON'T FAINT!

I still think of my daddy and my biological father daily. But, my thoughts are now thoughts of hope and adoration, and not of sorrow. I have accepted God's plan for my life and understand that my story itself, has a purpose, and it is not about me. It was written in the beginning of time that I would be chosen and set aside to be different. He knew before He formed me in my mother's womb what He planned for me during this life; only, I am just now coming into this knowing. But delayed, is not denied.

There is still time to tell your story. There is still time for you to seek healing in every broken relationship. There is still time for you to find yourself in Him and become whole and no longer be broken or bound – if you want the Promise bad enough. Know that you cannot afford to escape the pressure and run from the pain. Your promise will be aborted if you do and you will die and leave this earth with gifts buried and your soul full of grief, simply because you did not take the time and fulfill your destiny according to God's plan and His divine purpose.

Will it be easy? No.

Will it hurt at times, Yes.

Will it be worth it – absolutely.

Something you already know but need to remember:

1. God created you for a purpose.
2. You have gifts inside of you – use them.
3. You are not a mistake.
4. You are destined for greatness.
5. You have a story to tell that will bring about healing, tell it!
6. You are fearfully and wonderfully made.
7. You are the apple of God's eye.
8. You are the head and not the tail.
9. You are above and not beneath.
10. You were created to be great – so BE what you were created to BE, to be anything less, is an insult to God and a disservice to yourself.

PRESSURE...PAIN..PROMISE.

She cried her last tear at the Altar,

There, she laid down her burdens and all of her pain -

Never again

to be touched by her, as

She left them with her Father -

The One who promised to wipe her tears away.

And He did

And left no residue upon her.

She had a peace now,

that she could not explain -

She had unspeakable joy

That took pride in replacing her pain.

She was ready to love

Because she now loved herself.

She realized she was searching for a father that

In reality,

Never left.

Her void was filled

By the Alpha and the

Omega

And He loved her -

More than life.

A JOURNEY FROM DARKNESS TO DESTINY

Letter from the Author...

To the 14,000+ children in Florida,

And countless children all over the world

who remain in Foster Care

Longing for their Forever families...

To the many children who have been adopted and wonder why...

Stay encouraged and know that you were never abandoned,

Nor, were you thrown away,

You are special,

You, my beloved, are

Chosen...

Always Remember:

Tell Your Story –

Even if your voice shakes.

www.PressurePainPROMISE.com